To Be A GRADUATE

PRESENTED TO

_____

ON

_____ , 19_____

To Be A GRADUATE
by RUTH VAUGHN

THOMAS NELSON PUBLISHERS
NASHVILLE/NEW YORK

All rights reserved under International and Pan-American Conventions. Published in Nashville, Tennessee, by Thomas Nelson Inc., Publishers and simultaneously in Don Mills, Ontario, by Thomas Nelson & Sons (Canada) Limited. Manufactured in the United States of America.

Library of Congress Cataloging in Publication Data

Vaughn, Ruth.
   To be a graduate.

   1. Christian life—1960-   2. Vaughn, Ruth.
I. Title.
BV4501.2.V37   248'.2 [B]   79-1404
ISBN 0-8407-4073-5

To Be A
GRADUATE

What Is It To Be A Graduate?

What is it to be a graduate?

It is to be in recovery from the horror of final exams.

It is to be in shock at the dignity of academic regalia that is self-fitted.

It is to be in trepidation of the challenges that loom in the distance—alien, awesome, ahead.

What is it to be a graduate?

It is to be a nostalgic looking back at the past with all its loves, hates, successes, failures, aspirations, and memories.

It is to be a visionary looking toward the future with the dream of all it may hold.

It is to be a realist standing at the crossroads where past and future meet and fuse in the spotlight on the present.

What is it to be a graduate?

It is to stand on a pinnacle and perceive the fluidity of life: its flow of dailiness up to this moment of triumph; its flow from this moment back into dailiness.

It is to stand before a long corridor of doors whose opening or remaining closed is now a personal choice.

It is to stand at a corner knowing that once the T U
R
N

is made, life will never be the same again.

A Voice speaks through the inner rioting:
"Graduate, T U
R
N with Me.

I know new roads that lead to new worlds that will be best for the uniqueness of *you,* if *you* dare to follow Me."

New roads! New worlds! God-chosen! What a dare!

The Voice beckons: "Let Me pilot and we'll explore them together."

What is it to be a Graduate?

It is to hear the Lord of all creation daring you to follow His lead from the known into the unknown, from the tried into the untried, from the conquered into the unconquered.

It is to know that the Creator, Preserver, Redeemer, Almighty Sovereign loves you enough to fling the challenge—to reach higher than you think you can attain, to persevere more courageously than you think you can achieve, to be bigger than you think you can be.

It is to poise at the Beginning of Becoming . . . with God.

What Is It To Poise At The Beginning Of Becoming With God

Life is not a series of chances.

Life is a series of *choices.*

You did not choose all that *has happened* to you, nor will you choose all that *will happen* to you. You *will* choose your reaction to those events. You *will* choose the effect of those events. You *will* choose whether you face them alone or with God.

As you stand at the crossroads where the past and the future fuse into the present, you *can* choose your own roads, your own worlds, to be self-piloted. That can be your choice.

But as you stand at the crossroads, pause to consider. Does it not make sense that the Creator-God could guide you, His creation, on roads leading to worlds that would be more fulfilling to the God-created uniqueness of you than any road or any world you could choose for yourself?

He knows *who* you are.

He knows *why* you are.

He is your best Guide.

If you choose to let Him pilot your life, you will have made a major decision. But there are many elements in your releasing self-will into other hands. Each of these have to be understood and explored if the dimension of God's leadership is to be complete.

9

Perhaps the psalmist David best articulated life-commitment in all of its specific components in Psalm 23. I find Leslie F. Brandt's *Psalms/Now* paraphrase to be the most helpful.

This provides a framework to explore all that is involved in Beginning to Become.

PSALM 23

The Lord is my constant companion.
There is no need that He cannot fulfill.
Whether His course for me points
    to the mountaintops of glorious ecstasy,
    or to the valleys of human suffering,
    He is by my side,
    He is ever present with me.
He is close beside me
    when I tread the dark streets of danger,
    and even when I flirt with death itself,
    He will not leave me.
When the pain is severe,
    He is near to comfort.
When the burden is heavy,
    He is there to lean upon.
When depression darkens my soul,
    He touches me with eternal joy.
When I feel empty and alone,
    He fills the aching vacuum with His power.
My security is in His promise
    to be near to me always,
    and in the knowledge
        that He will never let me go.*

The Lord Is My Constant Companion

It was my crossroads.

My home-secure, love-certain past was behind. The future with its beckon to dream fulfillment, goal achievement, and maturity attainment lay before me.

I understood the adventure of the challenging new world; I could see its beauty sparkling on the horizon; I could hear the laughter of those who were finding their peace; I could feel the excitement whirling by on every breeze. A part of me wanted to rush into the new world, fling wide my arms, and embrace it all in a single moment!

Another part of me wanted to rush quickly back home, bury my head under my familiar pillow, and remain . . . forever.

My father was beside me.

Although an unusually eloquent minister behind a pulpit, he became a shy, awkward, inarticulate father when confronting a beloved child. We both shuffled our feet, polished spots on the car, and let the silence tumult between us.

Finally the moment came when he *had* to climb into the car and drive away, leaving me to face my new world alone. His voice husky, he made only one statement. I have never forgotten it.

11

"Whenever you are afraid of a thing, you are basically in doubt about God's interest in it with you, and that's unfair . . . to you and to Him."

Quickly we spoke our last love-words. He got into the car beside my mother and drove away.

As I watched them turn the corner to return to the scene of my past, I knew that when I turned, I would be in the midst of my future. In the space of that heartbeat, life would never be the same for me again.

When I got to my college dormitory room, the beginning of the flood of tears halted abruptly when I stopped to think of what he had said, "Whenever you are afraid of a thing, you are basically in doubt about God's interest in it with you, and that's unfair . . . to you and to Him."

Was that true: Was I in doubt about God's concern?

In the blinding panic of stepping into a strange "new world," filled with unknown customs, untried demands, unfamiliar people . . . had I forgotten that *I was not alone?*

True . . . it *was* a new world.

True . . . my parents . . . my friends . . . my *known* were not with me here . . . so had I, then, assumed that I *was* alone?

Honestly searching my heart, I discovered that was true. My fear stemmed from two major factors: (1) loneliness and (2) insecurity.

Now . . . if I knew, beyond question, that the God who had created me and had been *with* me in every moment of life's evolvement was *with* me now, then . . . I was not alone.

That took care of factor 1.

Moreover, if I knew, beyond question, that the God who had created the universe, of which this particular locale was only an infinitesimal part, was *with* me and *interested* in each facet of my "new world," ready to guide me through the alien maze of customs, demands, faces, then I was not without security.

That took care of factor 2.

Of course, there would be the added flow of adrenaline in the challenge of discovery and adjustment. The anxiety of doing my best would cause stomach-flutters, palm-moistening, fear-gasps. But if I *knew* I was accompanied by a God who was as interested in my fulfillment as I . . . then there would be no need for stomach-STOMPS, palm-FLOODS, and fear-SCREAMS.

"The Lord is my constant companion" . . . I have no need of fear!

I stood and walked to the window. The "new world" unreeled before my eyes . . .

I smiled . . .

shakily . . .

but I smiled. The tension was beginning to ease. It was my "new world," but I was not alone!

"The Lord is my constant companion" calmed the wild beating of my heart as I poised at the Beginning of Becoming . . . with God!

There Is No Need That He Cannot Fulfill

It was my life.

I looked it over carefully, studied its dimensions, and mapped out the road I wanted to follow. When I was

13

finished, I was immensely self-pleased. I noted every dream-fulfillment ... every goal-achievement ... every need-satisfaction ... and then I handed the finished life-map to God and asked for His approval.

He handed it back.

He said: "No."

Shocked, I jumped from my chair in a rage. Surely I had the *right* to chart my course! I paced the floor, shouting questions, hurling epithets, flooding tears.

When the explosion subsided, I sagged back into my chair and shut up. In the stillness, I heard that still small Voice challenging:

"T U
R
N with Me. I know new roads that lead to new worlds that will be best for the uniqueness of you, if you dare to follow Me."

I shrank back. It would be so much nicer to simply follow the road map that I could chart from my youthful human view.

Yes, I had to admit ... God's plans would surely be higher and finer than mine. But they would be so demanding ... so commanding ... so ... *stretching!*

I felt much more secure with my self-made plan.

The Voice came again: "Let Me pilot and we'll explore new worlds and new roads together."

What a dare!

God-piloted? My hands off?

"But God," I cried, "... how can I be sure?"

"I mean ... what about money ... family obligations ... all the *needs* of my life ... have You thought about *that?*"

14

His eye, I remembered from the biblical record, is on the sparrow . . . that small fluttery brownness.

Imagine! The tiny sparrow . . . of almost no value to anyone . . . is under the constant surveillance of the Creator-God!

"Fear ye not therefore," the Voice spoke again to my youthful quaking heart, "ye are of more value than many sparrows."*

Ah yes!

If He cared for the needs of the sparrows would He not care for the needs of His beloved child?

"Yes," but still my heart questioned. "Yes, but do You know that I have a need for love, giving/receiving, achievement . . . do You know?"

"I created you."

That stopped me short.

Every need was placed in my heart at the time of creation. My personality-uniqueness was not merely a freakish accident of developing cells. I was divinely designed for God-use in the world.

All of the dreams that needed fulfillment . . .

All of the goals that needed achievement . . .

All of the desires that needed satisfaction . . . were God-placed.

Only in following His lead onto "new roads" into "new worlds" could those needs possibly be met. Only the Creator would understand the precise dimension of each need . . . Only the Creator would know *how* to fulfill.

"And all the money, the food and clothes, the mental capabilities, the social acceptance, the shampoo and socks . . . You *will* supply?"

*Matt. 10:31

15

His Voice sounded amused: "Remember the sparrow."

Yes, I am of more value than many sparrows.

My needs are not my own. They are *ours* because there are always two of us involved: I, the created.

God, the Creator.

What a magnificent fact!

In that understanding, there can never be fear!

"There is no need that He cannot fulfill" gave me the courage to let go of self-made plans and give myself to the glory of divine-charting as I poised at the Beginning of Becoming . . . with God!

Whether His Course For Me Points . . .

It was my life-map.

It was tangible, static, safe. Set down to insure all my wants-supplied, it went from point-to-point-to-point in a predetermined manner. But I had to give it up.

I agreed to follow the Creator-God wherever He might lead. I quickly learned that such guidance held few parallels to my original direction. God's plan was more challenging, more demanding, and more frightening than I had imagined.

I had chosen a major in college.

I had chosen the person I wanted to marry.

I had chosen a career I would like to follow.

And God pushed all of those aside and said: "Follow
Me. I know new roads that lead to new worlds if
you T U

    R

   N with Me."

I was terrified.

Questions came forth from my quaking heart with
the power and intensity of bombs being dropped. Their
explosions were tearing up all that held certainty for me.

"What if the major You choose is too difficult for me?
What if my competence is insufficient? The major I chose
is an easy one for me. What if I follow You and *fail?*"

"What if I refuse to marry the young man of my
choice and no one ever asks me again! I want love, mar-
riage, children. What if I follow You and *live alone?*"

"What if the career You call me to reach for is beyond
me? What if my mental and creative capabilities are in-
adequate? What if I follow You and *fail?*"

The roar of the bombs finally ceased. In the silence, I
heard Him say: "I know new roads that lead to new worlds
that will be best for the uniqueness of you, if you will dare
to follow Me."

I shivered.

I was being led out of the known, shaken out of my
security, frightened out of my skin. . .

It was my life-map . . . and I would have no control
over its destination . . .

          over its charting . . .

               over its journeys. . .

                   what a dare!

My father used to say: "God can choose a plan for
your life that will please you better than any plan you can

choose for yourself." Note he did not say "would please God better." That is true, but he said, "will please *you* better than any plan you can choose for yourself."

Indeed, my father, who had self-chosen to be a farmer, had proven it true in following God's leading into a divine-chosen pulpit ministry.

My friend, Lindy, was then proving it true after giving up her self-map leading to a ballerina's life and following a God-map that had led directly into a children's hospital where she was completing an internship.

On the list could run . . . nice stories . . . true stories . . . but still stories about *other* lives. I was still looking at the precious self-map of *my* life. Giving its treasure into other hands . . . abandoning all control of its destination and turns . . . was *my* dare.

I looked at my point-to-point-to-point life-map. I *could* choose this major; I *could* marry this man; I *could* enter this career. That option was mine.

And therein lay security.

But I had heard a higher calling.

"I know new roads that lead to new worlds that will be best for the uniqueness of you, if you will dare to follow Me."

I took a deep breath . . . and *dared*!

My father had said: "God can choose a plan for your life that will please you better than any plan you can choose for yourself." I would set out to prove his maxim.

I would reach out to touch God's hand . . .

I would dare to follow . . . "Whether His course for me points. . ."

I could feel something shifting deep inside . . .

I was Beginning to Become . . . with God!

To The Mountaintops
Of Glorious Ecstasy

It was my wave-crest!
New roads. . .
Leading to new worlds. . .
He had promised that . . . and when I dared to follow,
wouldn't you know it . . . *there they were!*
Beautiful as dreams-come-true!
Throbbingly real as Truth Himself!

    I wasn't failing in God's plan for me . . .
    I wasn't dateless . . .
    I was Spirit-filled . . .
        Joy-intoxicated . . .
            Achievement-bedazzled . . .
I raced in the world where maples burned with color,
              willow trees let down their soft
                green hair,
              mountains showed forth their
                tresses of waterfalls,
              hummingbirds darted and
                reeled,
              the cockerel sun climbed
                aloft,
              steeping in sweetness its
              beams of light . . .

19

and a tiny redbird opened his heart in a crescendo that chimed like the tinkle of a heavenly bell . . . and I knew that God *is* Love . . . that the Creator is wiser than I . . . that all things *do* work together for good for those who love God.

My heart bulged with the joy of it all.

And I knew, with unshakable certainty, that there are always two involved in my life: God, the Creator,

I, the created . . .

I had nothing to fear!

The Almighty is *interested* in every phase of my life.

Every need He will fulfill.

Not a single phase of the adventure lies outside His loving jurisdiction.

I will never walk alone!

Such glory we shared that day . . .

the heavenly Father and I . . .

and I penned

a song on the flyleaf of my Bible to triumphantly preserve the moment.

Whirl in the carousel of His dizzying colors . . .
Jump in the ballet of His dancing waters . . .
Swing on the emerald vines of His towering oaks . . .
AND TOUCH THE HAND OF GOD!

Explore in the firecrackers of His golden lightning . . .
Shout in the chorus of His multi-harmonic winds . . .
Tiptoe in the wonder of His many-splendored rainbow . . .
AND TOUCH THE HAND OF GOD!

Leap to the majesty of His Incredible skies . . .
Twirl notes of music with His Inimitable mockingbird . . .
Reach out in the glory of His sun . . .
AND TOUCH THE HAND OF GOD!

20

As the blue, plum-colored dusk drowned the pomegranate-red sun, the whole world became hushed in wonder. I leaned against the night, listening to the small sonatas of the tree-leaves, watching the horned, mischievous moon tiptoeing on the threshold of the cobalt night; and my being ached with the marvel of sharing *all this* with Him!

I poised at the Beginning of Becoming . . . and knew the "mountaintops of glorious ecstasy . . ." with God!

Or To The Valley Of Human Suffering

It was my ocean bottom.

After my moment of agonizing commitment to follow God's direction instead of my own life-map . . .

After daring to believe the Creator-God was *with* me and *interested* in fulfilling all my God-designed needs . . .

My footsteps had trippingly scampered to the mountaintops of ecstasy and I had reveled in the reality of His presence . . . exulted in the truth of His promises . . . and unquestionably *knew* that my choice was right!

With the triumph of my joy-song leaping crescendo from my happy heart . . . we began to move again . . .

I noted we were descending . . . and the terrain began to change.

A cold wind swaggered by, shouldering me roughly as it passed. Thunder turned from major chords to minor

21

wails and soon became vociferous like angry wolves growling over dark, frosty bones. Ice froze the rippling waters, transforming them into brightly scoured armor plate. The birds were gone. The sun had set. All became dark and frightening.

Still we descended.

I had heard of valleys. I had no idea how *deep* a valley could be, or how painful.

I had realized that life with God could not always be lived on the mountaintops of ecstasy. I determined to be brave in facing the valleys of human suffering, and I thought surely my reward would soon come.

But disappointment topped disappointment. Nothing went the way I had planned. Confusion tore at me with mad-dog teeth.

And then my brother came.

He told me my mother had been hospitalized. The diagnosis was Parkinson's disease, an incurable illness.

The maturity for which I strained in the presence of others completely dissolved when I got alone with God.

"What are You doing?" I screamed. "This was not included in my releasing life to You. When I charted my life-map, there was no place for incurable illness in my beloved mother. Now ... following You ... I find this torture-point hurled into my life like a flaming arrow, burning away all the joy and security I have known.

"This wasn't in our bargain," I sobbed to the Creator. "I never wanted to know sorrow like this!"

The torrent of tears raged over me. I yelled, cried, and pounded my fists until I lay completely exhausted at His feet. In the silence, I heard Him gently speak:

"I never promised that if you would walk with Me, you would never know the valley of suffering. My promise was that when you trod the valley of suffering, you would not be alone."

Slowly my contorting muscles stilled.

"I am here. My grace is sufficient for all your needs."

I was silent for a long while . . . trying to think it through.

It had been so easy to believe in God's wisdom when I flitted on the mountaintops of ecstasy. . .

It was hideously more difficult now that I shivered in the tumultuous storm in the valley of human suffering. But was that fair?

I was afraid of suffering.

I was afraid of helplessness.

I was afraid of life that did not go according to my specifications.

It was so *easy* to see God's interest, feel His presence, believe His wisdom in the sunshine. Everything was beautiful and glowing then.

> Just like the times I had run
> through the meadows with my kite-
> string tightly clasped in my
> hand as I did sky-dances with
> God's wind . . .
> How *close* He had been to me then!

But I remembered that there had been other times in my past when everything was murky and terrifying.

> Just like the time I had hidden
> in the cellar behind packing
> boxes, determined to remain there
> until I died because I had knocked
> a baseball through the window of

my father's shiny new car . . .
How *close* God had been to me then!

Yes, He had.

In that damp, dank, dusty basement, I had shivered in my fear and felt that God huddled there with me . . . just as He was with me now.

These recent disappointments were more life-vital than my third-grade pep-club-tryouts.

My mother's incurable illness was more devastating than the broken window of my father's shiny new car.

But as He had been with me in the past . . . so was He with me now.

I took a deep breath.

The loving Redeemer God would provide adequate grace, strength, and courage to make even these unpleasant, even tragic, events "work together for good" because I did love God . . . because He *was* in control of all of my life.

To allow fear to overwhelm me was unfair—to me because of the price I paid in anguish, bitterness, and anger . . . to God because He had proven Himself to be worthy of my trust.

Poised at the Beginning of Becoming . . . I found security for all of life's storms, no matter how unexpected,
how unpleasant,
how upheaving,
for I found His presence sufficient . . . even in the valleys of human suffering. . .

What a vital,
valuable,
victorious,
reality in the Beginning of Becoming . . . with God!

He Is By My Side

It was my self-discovery.

I had heard it all my life. I had even practiced it all my life. But somehow, until that crisis-time in the valley of human suffering, I had never allowed its meaning to become my own.

God is by my side.

Early in my life, my mother had told me about Brother Lawrence, the French Carmelite monk who went about his work among the pots and pans of his monastery "practicing the presence of God" every moment. As a high schooler, I had read his tiny book and used it for a class book report. Some of its archaic phrases had emblazoned themselves on my heart and were mine forever.

Now as I stood in my lonely room on a college campus, hundreds of miles from the hospital where my mother lay with an incurable illness, I cried out a prayer jerked from the human heart of Brother Lawrence centuries before. When facing some terrible impossibility, he had whispered to the Lord: "I cannot do this unless Thou enablest me."

Between my sobs, I now sputtered the same succinct confession of my helplessness. "I cannot do this unless Thou enablest me."

I could hear the smile in His Voice as He said quietly, down where the meanings are, "I know."

Somehow those two words began to dam the flood of tears.

He *knew*.

He, whom I loved,

He, whom I had proven faithful in all of life's circumstances,

He, who was the almighty Sovereign of the universe, was *with* me . . . *interested* in every facet of my life . . . and He *knew* I could not face the valleys of human suffering *unless He enabled me!*

I remembered: "Your helplessness leads you to My sufficiency." He had known, every moment of my life, that I could never grow up to be strong enough to face life's tragedies unless He enabled me. That is why He had said: "Let me pilot and we'll explore . . . together."

Together.

Therein lay my strength.

Like the shock of an electric current, the truth I had learned when I had turned my life over to God reverberated through my every corpuscle. There are always two of you involved: God, the Creator
You, the created.

All my faith . . . all my life experiences to this point . . . all Scripture . . . was not merely theory, illusion, and wishful thinking. For the first time, my mind grappled with the *fact* that I was *not* alone . . . not when I rejoiced on the mountaintops . . . not when I sorrowed in the valleys.
Until this moment, I had *reacted* . . . gliding by on the superficial layers of life with God. Now I determined to begin to bore down for bedrock that would give me

strength in *all* of life, so I could *act* and *move* with purpose.

The key, I knew, lay in Brother Lawrence's concept of "practicing the presence of God" every moment. He had done so among his pots and pans in a monastery. My mother had done so in a bare-floored parsonage filled with eight children. I would do so in academia beset with books and term papers and final exams.

Thus I began my conscious effort of "practicing His presence" so that the internalizing of the truth: "He is by my side" would be thorough, lasting, immovable.

I awoke in the morning and whispered:

> Good morning, God,
> The day is new;
> Please help me to use it all
> For You.

Mentally, I focused on His presence in walking to class. I breathed a prayer as I began to try to comprehend the difficult lecture presented. In odd moments of class conversation, I would write short prayers in shorthand to God in the margins of my paper. Wherever I went, I was aware that He paced with me. Whenever I pondered, I was sensitive to His meditating with me. However I felt, I was certain He understood.

"Thank You."

"Give me wisdom."

"Be *with* me now!"

"Help, please!"

All these became flash-prayers that constantly were transmitted to my ever-present Friend.

At night, with my head on my pillow, my last thoughts were:

> Good night, dear God.
> Thank You for the day.
> I love You, God,
> More than I can say.

Soothing, comforting, healthy rest enfolded me like a warm blanket as He gave "His beloved sleep."
Every moment . . .
Every day . . .
mountaintops of ecstasy . . .
valleys of human suffering . . .
waking refreshed in the morning . . . working,
studying,
playing,
achieving,
sleeping soundly at night . . . "He is by my side!"
Interested in every phase of my life . . .
Nothing too small to fall outside His loving concern,
No reason to *ever* be afraid!
Exulting, I cried in the throb of truth:
There are always two of you involved:
God, the Creator
You, the created!
What glory to poise at the Beginning of Becoming . . . with the ever-present, ever-interested, ever-loving God!

He Is Ever-Present With Me

It was the first letter from my mother after the
T U
  R
N into the new world of the future.

As was typical for her, it began with lines from a poet unknown to me. They were:

> Let your bending in the Archer's
> hand be for gladness;
>
> For even as he loves the arrow that
> flies, so he loves also the bow
> that is stable.

As the youngest child in my family, my home-tie-breaking ended the guardian role of my parents. But the lines following the verse reflected their courage:

> There will be no tears tonight,
> for we, your father and I, now rest
> from our past role as the Creator's bow.
> You, His own unique arrow,
> must find your personal way,
> evolve your personal faith,
> follow your personal star.
> Our prayer is that you shall go
> swift and far.

As the newly-flung arrow, I lodged in a world of four dimensions very different from the warm cocoon of my parents' simple faith. After only a few weeks, my mind whirled with theories of degree and relativity and Einstein's proof that matter is energy and energy, matter . . . Seconds, minutes, hours, days, weeks, months, seasons, and years . . . measures in relation to the sun, the moon, and the stars. . . And man, during his brief time on earth, egocentrically orders in his mind the happenings: past, present, and future. And for the first time, I touched the quicksand of the theory that God is dead.

Experientially, I had proven it a lie.

Intellectually, I could not cope.

The confusion sucked me ever-nearer the drowning-point.

My searching, demanding mind had a revulsion against accepting anything other than total truth. In all my growing-up years, I had never been in a position of challenging the validity of God's existence.

Now confronting the thoughts of other men, I knew I had to question. Only in the crucible of honest testing could truth emerge whole.

What was man?

"The measure between the macro-universe and the micro-universe," someone said.

"Man is nothing else but what he makes of himself," wrote Jean-Paul Sartre.

"Men are God's beloved children," my father often stated behind the pulpit.

I shook my head in confusion. I admired the intellect of Sartre. I had read his writings for class assignments and felt my own inner drive for truth race with his.

But as I continued my perusal of Sartre, the more it

seemed to lead to frustration—a hall of mirrors and a hundred half-reflections of man, silent and alone.

In a world of billions of people, each one stands
> as one-of-a-kind,
> unique,
> never-before-on-earth,
> never-to-be-again . . .

And Sartre said: "Man is nothing else but what he makes of himself"?

Certainly Franklin Roosevelt, Helen Keller, Abraham Lincoln, Joan of Arc, and Ludwig Beethoven had aspired with vigor to be the best they could be . . . dreaming . . . thrust forward from the dream . . . testing and trying the new . . . failing and trying again . . . ever reaching for life's highest; but that indomitable vigor was what *man made of himself?*

I was incredulous.

That was lunacy.

I remembered a statement made by Helen Keller. When asked if she believed in God, she said: "Oh, I always knew Him. Every moment of every day, I knew Him. I just didn't know His name."

In the dark silence of her world
> where she never heard a word about creed,
> where she never learned a single catechism,
> where no human person influenced her thoughts. . .

she *knew* the divine Personality who was with her every moment of every day.

In the dark. . .

In the silence. . .

In the human loneliness. . .

She *knew* the Almighty.

31

She just didn't know His name.

"Jean-Paul Sartre," my mind spoke out, "I commend your searching intellect; I reject your conclusions."

In our human talent, operating independently, we may build our towers of Babel to the clouds. . .

We may contrive ingeniously to circumvent nature by devices of great complexity . . .

We may rummage the whole planet for ease and comfort . . .

But it is of no avail unless there is *something more* than what man can make of himself!

Ah, no! I could not intellectually buy the idea of man as an accidental collection of cells wandering vaguely about waiting for death to end it all. Just as the miracle of the universe demanded an intelligent Creator-God . . . so did the miracle of man, both physically and spiritually speaking, command a supreme Creator-God.

Intellectually I could not *but* believe.

There was *something more* than mental faith: There was experiential knowledge.

As a child I had sat in the top of my mulberry tree, holding my doll tightly to my breast, whispering secret dreams,

poems,

and fantasies

to an unseen Personality who, I felt with certainty, was sharing with me.

I had raced down a country road as a teen-ager, singing lustily: "I love life and I want to live!" and knew with assurance that an unseen Personality exulted with me.

I had stood at life's crossroads between past and future and felt the dynamics of an unseen Personality daring me to find new roads into new worlds designed for the uniqueness of *me* . . . and had confident perception that He was Truth.

After my first exposure to Sartre . . . to theories of relativity . . . to questions of logic . . . I found the reality that "He is ever-present with me. . . ." And I felt my spirit surge with peace as I poised at the Beginning of Becoming . . . with God.

He Is Close Beside Me

It was my daily choice . . .
> to believe in the reality of God.
> to believe in the wisdom of God
> to believe in the love of God.

But I discovered an unexpected choice . . . the dimension of His participation in my life.

Just as He would not take control of my life without my *choosing* to ask Him . . . and *choosing* to give Him full power . . . just so He would never work in the daily nitty-gritty circumstances of human life without my *choosing* to allow Him.

This first began to dawn on me when I faced injustice face-to-face.

It was an essay contest. The subject was "What Democracy Means to Me." The promotor was a well-known

33

business firm. The prize was a trip to the U.S. capital in Washington, D.C.

I had written a theme on that subject in high school composition class. On an impulse, I decided to polish and expand it for an entry. I was notified by mail that I had won.

In jubilation, I went to the business office at the appointed time. The lady who received me wore a glacier smile and her manner froze my animation into immobility.

I listened to the goals she had in mind for the trip. The feeling intensified that I had no part in them. Finally she whipped out a sheet of paper and handed it to me.

My eyes slid across its contents. 1. formal
　　　　　　　　　　　　　　　2. dinner dresses
　　　　　　　　　　　　　　　3. party dresses
I had no wardrobe of these specifications. I could not ask my parents to buy me one.

I noted the triumph in her icy eyes as she said: "You will comply with the clothing requirements, will you not?"

I hesitated, frowning, not knowing what to say.

And then I understood, for she said in her steel-brittle voice, "If you can't, we will be glad to replace you."

Ah! For some reason Miss Glacier wanted to replace me. I couldn't imagine why. They had not had to choose my essay. I knew it was one of hundreds. So why choose it if they did not want me?

Then the rattle of Miss Glacier's ice-cube voice began to come through . . .

"We really don't think a minister's daughter is representative of the entire population. . ."

"A small religious college does not produce a mentality representative of the entire state. . ."

"You couldn't possibly have the sophistication necessary for the representation needed. . ." So!

34

The essay had obviously been chosen by some literary committee, but when the business firm was confronted with the person who wrote the essay, they were embarrassed. I suppose they had envisioned a Hollywood starlet. Sitting in the winner's chair was a diminutive Miss Average dressed in plaid skirt, bright-colored sweater, grey loafers. They wanted someone else.

I handed the paper back to her and got up.

"I cannot accept the trip," I told her.

Just as I had informed no one of my entering the contest, so I now informed no one of its results. Life moved on, but the hard knot of bitterness grew tighter and the wall of resentment grew higher and I found myself changing for the worse.

One late afternoon, I sat in my room wallowing in self-pity, anger, hostility . . . when my best friend whirled in with the news that I had made an A on a major test. When I didn't respond, she asked, "What's the matter with you? Are you mad at me?"

"Of course not," I told her impatiently. She had a bubbly disposition that made everyone love her. "I've just discovered how *unjust* life can be! I don't want to talk about it."

She laughed.

"Why are you laughing?" I asked her.

"So you've discovered injustice! Is that all?"

"ALL!"

I exploded. "ALL! What do you mean . . . ALL!"

"But whoever told you life would always be fair?" she asked with the disarming frankness I found so endearing.

I could not comprehend her careless acceptance. I was so stunned I was speechless. She kicked off her shoes, lay back on the bed, and studied her wiggling toes.

She made me feel like a small child, which only compounded my anger. I did not need the feeling of being ridiculous piled on top of my angry bitterness.

Finally she sat up. Her face was serious.

"Okay. I don't know who's kicked you in the stomach. I don't know why. But I do know how it feels. When I was six, my parents told me they were getting a divorce. I could choose whether to live on the East Coast with my mother or on the West Coast with my father. But ne'er the twain should meet!

"What an *unjust* decision to force upon a child. It ended up, of course, with my spending six months one place and six months another and never belonging anywhere."

She pulled my parents' picture from the desk. "Do you have any idea how I envy you? You reel off so casually the things you and your parents share . . . remember the story you tell of your parents taking you to Myers Creek where the three of you crept close to the water . . . your father began a bass song to which the bullfrogs joined in . . . and then you and your mother chimed in the song . . . and your family and the bullfrogs made music *together?*"

I nodded, smiling at the childhood story.

"The first time I heard you tell that episode, I thought my heart would explode. I left the room as quickly as I could because I was in tears. You were so *wealthy* and you didn't even know! I have *no* memories of that kind of love in my life. It was *wrong* that you should be given such a store of love-lined remembrances . . . when I had *none!* I went out onto the mall that night and cried. I hated you. I hated my parents. I hated life. I was full of despair. I despised the *injustice* of it all!"

"I cried that night on the mall because I was so full of anger at the injustice of not having a love-lined childhood like yours . . . and then I realized that I was not alone . . . God was with me, hurting with me, fully understanding me . . . and yearning to help.

"But He wouldn't until I asked Him."

"Did you?" I whispered.

"Yes," she smiled gently. "I told Him I couldn't forgive my parents for the pain they had brought me . . . and He said, 'I know.' "

I gasped.

Those were the same words I had felt Him whisper inside my spirit when I had painfully jerked out the words of Brother Lawrence: "I cannot do this unless Thou enablest me."

My friend was continuing with her story.

"Well . . . 'if You know,' I said to Him, 'does that mean I don't have to forgive them?' And He said, 'If you'll open yourself to Me, I'll forgive them through you.' "

"What does that mean?" I asked.

"Just that. I simply bowed my head and whispered: "I need Your help. I ask You to do what I cannot . . .""

She paused. Her eyes were filled with awe.

"It was like . . . like a releasing thaw . . . the rock-hard snowball inside me began to ooze slowly from its icy tension into soft mush and ultimately into a stream that slipped away, out of sight forever."

"You didn't hate them anymore?" I asked.

I could see the amazement in her eyes.

"I didn't hate them anymore. The wounds were still there, but I perceived they would heal. . . . I knew I would listen to more of your stories about singing at the pond . . .

and I would touch the scar . . . but I knew that it would *be* a scar . . . the wound was beginning, even then, to heal."

As soon as I could, I slipped down to the prayer chapel. I knelt at the small altar and the tears began.

"I know I've been wrong," I told Him. "First, I was angry because You allowed injustice to crash into my world. Second, I wanted to be exempt from suffering. Third, I gave Miss Glacier the power to challenge my feelings of self-value . . . the power to crush my life into depression . . . the power to choke out other joys.

"Most of all, I became afraid . . . afraid of pain like that . . . afraid of what the choice of others, the tragedies of life, and human circumstance can do to me! And when I became afraid, I was basically in doubt about Your interest in my life . . . and that was unfair . . . to me and to You. I'm sorry."

That much, at least, was honest, but there had to be more.

"I can admit my error and ask forgiveness. But, oh God, I *hate* Miss Glacier. . .

"I can't forgive her for making me feel so small and insignificant and unworthy and. . .

I stopped because He had said something.

Two words.

"I know."

I smiled.

He knew I was not strong enough to forgive Miss Glacier. But when I opened myself to Him, He would forgive through me.

And, kneeling in the dimly-lit chapel, I did.

And He did.

And the work was done.

38

"He is close beside me"
                              every moment of every day
                                        waiting to help me
make creative redemptive *use* of every circumstance of
life, even the unpleasant ones.

I have the daily *free choice* to determine whether to
keep my spirit frozen in a snowball of resentful unforgive-
ness or whether I will release the angry bitterness from my
clenched fists and allow Him to melt it all away in divine
power.

What blessed fact on which to set my feet as I poised
at the Beginning of Becoming . . . with God!

When I Tread The Dark Streets Of Danger

It was my own footsteps of experience.
It was God's plan.

The longer I lived under His lordship the more I
understood that He wanted me to climb to the threshold of
my faith, not with the opinions of others, but with my
personal findings. I was not to be a parrot. I was to be a
realist with both feet planted on an inner foundation I had
built with stones of my own agony.

I was no robot mechanically following Him from dot-
to-dot-to-dot. I was a beloved child tossing about the
divine gift of free choice with innocent abandon.

I had to learn for myself its glories . . . and its responsibilities. I had to confront in stark reality the freedom of my choice . . . and the inevitable consequences.

I suppose it began to formulate for me when I accepted a challenge given at the college to join a team to visit children's hospitals. Since drama was my forte, I clowned and performed Dr. Seuss stories with delight. It brought joy to the children's faces and I was glad.

There was one little girl whose name was Diana. She had long, silky, dark hair; perfect olive complexion, and the saddest eyes I had ever seen. I tried to out-do myself in her ward every time we went. It seemed it took extra effort to tease even a small smile.

But one day I saw Diana laughing at some crazy routine. When it was all over, I went to her and kissed her goodbye.

That week I mailed her a copy of the book containing the fable I had performed. She wrote me a thank you note and told me I would always be her best friend.

Tryouts for an all-campus play came and I was given the female lead. I was completely overwhelmed with the charm of the male lead, and life began to spin about on a carousel of multicolored, many-spangled, glorious-musical joy. I had no time for the hospital troupe any longer.

One afternoon I was called by the administrator of one of the children's hospitals. He asked if I could come to his office on a matter of urgency.

When I arrived, he handed me a small scrap of paper. On it, in childish scrawl, I found these words: "Ruth said she would be my friend. She made me laugh. She even sent me a book. But she never comes anymore. She didn't want to be my friend. Nobody does. And so I don't want to live."

My anguished eyes jumped to the man's face. He nodded at my mute question. "She tried suicide. We pumped her stomach. She's very angry with us. I thought perhaps you could help."

"Oh, I'll try!" I whispered. "I didn't know. . . I didn't mean. . . I had no idea. . ."

He gently touched my shoulder.

"She needed you more than you knew. These children often do. They want more of us than we can give . . ."

"Or choose to give," I said soberly. "Not more than I could have given. I just didn't think. . ."

"Don't blame yourself," the kind man told me.

He led me to Diana's room.

She wouldn't look at me at first.

I tried talking about the weather . . . the room with its yellow curtains . . . Dr. Seuss . . . and then she whirled at me. I was startled by the fire in her eyes.

"You lied!" she shrieked at me.

"No, Diana. No. . . I didn't lie. . . I . . ."

"You lied!" she insisted. "You said you would be my friend. You *said* it that last day you were here. You even wrote in that book: 'Your friend.' And it was a *lie!*"

She saw my bewilderment and scornfully turned away. "Leave me alone," she said.

After a long time, I found my voice.

"Diana," I said huskily, "I can see that I was wrong. I didn't mean to let you down . . ."

She snorted.

I continued, "That doesn't change the fact that I did. But I hope it helps a little to know that I didn't intentionally

41

go out of your life. I was your friend; I cared about you; I wanted your happiness; I wanted to help. I still feel all of those things. They have never changed."

"Then why didn't you come back?" asked the small voice.

"Because . . . I was cast in a play that took a lot of time,

I met a boy who captured all of my attention,

I became so excited about personal events that . . ."

I faltered, but she picked it up . . . "that you forgot about me."

Time will never quite erase the agony of that moment.

Diana ultimately forgave me. In spite of the play . . . in spite of the romance . . . in spite of a busy schedule, I faithfully visited that hospital ward until she was released to go back to her home in another state. We continue, even after all these years, to correspond. We *are* friends.

But that was, perhaps, the time when I was made most aware of the power that God had placed in my hands in the form of free choice.

I could *choose* to be faithful to others. . .
I could *choose* to be faithless.

I could *choose* to be genuine in my assertions. . .
I could *choose* to be artificial.

I could *choose* to be true to my ideals. . .
I could *choose* to be false.

42

I not only *could* choose . . . I *would* choose.

Unwittingly . . . unthinking . . . unaware of consequences . . . perhaps so; but I would still choose . . . and
the results would be the same as if they had been pre-
planned.

On my way home from the hospital that evening, I
remember coming to a Catholic church. I climbed its
steps, found its heavy door unlatched, and went inside.

It was an alien setting, but I could sense holiness
present.

I went to a rail and knelt.

"I know Your Ten Commandments; I know the
Beatitudes by memory," I whispered. "I have heard my
father preaching about all that is involved in living a holy
life, caring for others, being true to responsibility. My
mother has quoted poetry, sung songs, and heart-talked
with me about such things all my life. But it was just so
much *talk*. I didn't understand . . . till now. . .

"I didn't understand, in my own experience, the 'dark
streets of danger' on which You freely let me stride . . .

"Oh God!" my voice broke on a sob, "Oh God! I
cannot do this unless Thou enablest me."

And He said: "I know."

And I smiled.

It was becoming a familiar dialogue.

I am too weak to wend my way successfully in a world
where my gift of free choice has such awesome, far-
reaching consequences upon my destiny and upon
others' destinies.

So, in helplessness, I can ask for divine help . . . for
my helplessness leads me directly to *His* sufficiency.
Every time.

"He is by my side when I tread the dark streets of

danger." I am climbing to the threshold of my own perceptions not with the statement of others but with the footsteps of my own experience. With His constant presence, I can make the journey without fear. That knowledge enabled me to be open to responsibility as I poised at the Beginning of Becoming . . . With God!

And Even When I Flirt With Death Itself

It was my first real glimpse of death.

My grandfather had died when I was seven. But I hadn't known him. He lived in a distant city. We rarely visited. I knew him as a gracious silvery-haired gentleman who patted my curls and called me a "good girl." And although I sorrowed for my mother at his funeral, it was not a personal loss.

My boyfriend's grandfather had died when I was sixteen. I remember crying at his graveside where I stood with the family. But I had never seen the man before. I did not know true grief.

A high school chum had died the first semester of my freshman year at college. I mourned the loss of her life, but I was not notified until after the funeral, so it never became acutely real.

Except for those few vague brushes, death had stood apart from my life. I raced in the youthful vigor of overflowing activity and gave little thought to the fact that there would be termination.

And then it happened to me.

He had a yellow convertible, green eyes, and a rakish grin that could charm the most recalcitrant heart. He was my best friend's cousin, and he came to campus to show her a good time . . . and to impress her friends.

It was an easy job.

We crowded about him, laughed at his jokes, grew wide-eyed at his tales of adventure, and jumped with joy when he promised to take us for a ride in the yellow convertible. As we all piled into the car, he assured us it would be a ride we would never forget.

I haven't.

I doubt anyone else has.

Squealing his tires, he pulled away from the campus and headed the car toward a country road. Soon we were a wild streak of yellow careening through a sea of dusty foam.

I had never experienced such volatile motion. Probably none of the other girls had either. We shouted our approval. We laughed. We urged him on.

Sailing precipitously close to a ditch, he made a turn into a wooded area. We all shrieked with excitement as we realized he was going to weave in and out through the trees at top speed.

It was a riot of whirling, wheeling, whizzing fun . . . and then in a split-second we felt the car begin to slide. In terror we looked at our devil-may-care driver and saw his ashen face, his muscles working frantically on the unresponsive steering wheel, and we knew we were out of control.

The fast-spinning car was hurling toward a distant ditch, and we were powerless to stop its pace . . .

We could only stare in frozen fascination and feel death waiting.

Closer, closer came the abyss, and in a flying leap we felt ourselves in the air. We closed our eyes. There was a great jolt. A whirring noise. And finally . . . stillness.

Carefully, very carefully, we opened our eyes.

The car was clinging to the terrain of the other side of the ditch.

Breath returned slowly.

After a long while, someone whispered: "We should try to get out."

Gingerly, oh so gingerly, we began to climb out of the car and back away from it. When we were all free, we huddled together and looked at the up-tilted yellow car.

We gazed at it as if mesmerized. And then Jeanie articulated all our thoughts: "We could be dead now."

No one moved.

We were eighteen years old.

We had been laughing, shouting, exulting in whirling life. Then there was that crazy, heart-spinning second of a car-gone-wild. . .

Life wasn't the only fact. We knew now that death was a fact too.

My friend's green-eyed, charming cousin carefully climbed back into his car after awhile. He started the motor and was able to slowly back it across the ditch. We climbed into its leather interior in total silence.

He left us at the dormitory door with only the most succinct remarks. We girls went to the prayer chapel where we knelt in the stream of near-death encircling us all.

"We could be dead now," Jeanie had said.

It reeled in my brain.

It was truth.

And it would have come as a result of my own choice.

I had known from the regaled adventures that my best friend's cousin was a daring driver. I had cheered as he recounted his risks on freeways and hills. I had deliberately gotten into that car shouting for excitement.

One by one, my friends began to rise and slip out of the prayer chapel. Finally I was alone . . . with God . . . and I said aloud:

"Wow! What a powerful gift You placed in my hands when You gave me free choice . . ."

I remembered Diana. I shuddered.

"My choices affect the lives of others."

I remembered that screaming moment in space. I trembled.

"My choices affect my own destiny."

"Oh God!" I cried, "I am not wise enough to guide my life. I cannot do this unless Thou enablest me."

And I smiled in spite of the tears, for He simply said: "I know."

I was climbing higher daily, to the threshold of my own faith, not with the statements of others, but with the footsteps of my own experiential understanding: "He is close beside me when I tread the dark streets of danger and even when I flirt with death itself."

Thus I was free to let serenity roll back into my spirit, rise to my feet, and leave the prayer chapel in tranquility. Although I bore the choice of good and evil

even of life and death . . .

I could do so with courage, for *I was not alone* . . . not in the past . . . not in the future . . . not now, as I stood poised at the Beginning of Becoming . . . with God!

47

He Will Not Leave Me

It was my guilt.

I carried it wherever I went.

It never left my subconscious.

Even in class, I would pause in the midst of note-taking to scribble prayers in the margins of my paper: "Forgive me." In shorthand, I wrote it as one curlicued figure. It appeared so frequently on my pages that my friends complimented me on my decorations.

They did not know that the curlicue was not created for beauty; it was created out of pain.

It was Diana. Her attempted suicide because of my neglect had shaken me deeply.

That event, so quickly followed by the car-flying confrontation with death, had catapulted me into an abyss of self-blame, self-hatred, self-flagellation that never ceased.

I went to see Diana faithfully.

I sent her flowers, candy, and more Dr. Seuss books.

I rejoined the hospital troupe and gave all my verve to performing at every call.

My studies continued with my characteristic earnestness.

My romance blossomed into greater beauty.

Another play began rehearsals.

One night I sat on the back steps of the fine arts

building, concentrating on memorizing lines. As I whispered the words to myself, my pen was drawing a familiar shorthand figure all over the playbook cover.

The stage manager cued me to prepare to go on stage. As I went up the steps to the stage, the blue-eyed blonde, holder-of-my-heart, was coming off. I thrust the playbook into his hands and, with a toss of my head, whirled onto the stage in a flurry of memorized lines . . . and then . . . I fumbled. . .

The stage was spinning . . . I saw the director leap to his feet . . . and that was all.

I fainted center stage.

The school nurse lived across the street from the campus. The director sent for her. By the time she arrived, I was coming to. She patted my cheeks, rubbed my wrists, and declared that I was exhausted. She thought I should not rehearse anymore.

The director agreed and cancelled rehearsal.

Apologizing with due modesty, I bade my farewells and the charming blonde took my arm to escort me home. He was oddly silent all the way across the campus. But I was weary and did not mind.

When we went inside the dormitory parlor, he guided me to a sofa and we sat. He thrust the playbook into my hands.

"What does that mean?" he asked.

I looked down at the cover thoroughly bedecked with my shorthand scrawls. I laughed.

"It's shorthand."

"I can see that," he said quietly. "What does it mean?"

"Well . . ." I was hedging. "Well . . . it's a prayer."

"I thought so," he affirmed. "Now tell me what it means."

"Why did you think it was a prayer?"

His smile was gentle. "Because I know you," he said. "Now tell me: What is the prayer?"

My fingers traced the curves of the figure. "It reads like this, noble sir: For . . . give . . . me."

"And you have to pray that prayer that many times just on the cover of the playbook?"

I dropped my head.

"And you pray it all over the margins of your class notes. I've observed that for weeks now. And when we bow to pray together, there is an intensity about you that concerns me."

My eyes filled with tears.

I turned away, fighting for control.

He didn't move but his voice was softly compassionate. "Ruth, when I first heard about Diana, I knew your sensitive, conscientious spirit was going to take a beating. When you got back from that bout with the crazy stunt driver, I knew your responsibility-awareness was compounded. Because you are so sincere, you feel you must pay for your misjudgments. You cannot forgive yourself. You refuse to believe God forgives you."

Tears were now spilling uncontrollably. I turned back to look into his blue eyes: "Diana could have died . . .
because of my choice

"I could have died . . . because of my choice."

"But you're forgiven," he whispered. "That's over. You learned from both incidents. Now release it. Accept forgiveness. From God and from yourself."

He picked up the playbook.

"You don't have to live in strain pleading with God.

50

Ruth, He *wants* to forgive. He forgave the first time you asked. All these other hundreds of times per-page have been totally unnecessary."

"Oh Bill," I sobbed. "If only I could believe that!"

He tipped my chin. "Believe it. It's truth. You *know* it. You just won't let Him in."

He picked the playbook up from the sofa and handed it to me. "Let God forgive you once and for all." He held up the cover. "Release yourself from this senseless strain."

As I slowly started up the stairs, I decided to take his advice. Instead of going to my room, I went to the prayer chapel. I knelt in its dimly-lit interior and let my head sag in total weariness on the altar. My eyes beheld the shorthand-covered playbook on my lap. I did not say a word. But I closed my eyes in submission and I felt Him shatter the barrier with one gesture of love.

"I will not leave you," He said.

I was so tired of the strain.

I was so relieved to have Him enfolding me with tenderness.

I did not open my eyes as I whispered: "You will not leave me . . .

> even when I'm unwise,
> even when I'm untrue,
> even when I'm foolish?"

I could feel the warmth invading the frozen chambers of my heart as He responded, deep inside where the meanings are: "Even when!"

Tears trickled slowly, softly, gently down my cheeks and onto the playbook. The inked curliques began to smudge. It didn't matter. I didn't need them anymore.

Still sagging with deep weariness, I looked at my

fallible humanity . . . the challenge to become the fulfillment of God's creation-dream . . . and I whispered: "I
cannot do this unless Thou enablest me."

And we both smiled as He responded: "I know."
Either deliberately or inadvertantly I may be unwise, uncar-
ing, immoral, but He will not leave me . . . even when!
Slowly . . . so very slowly . . . I began to truly *trust* His
constant presence as I stood poised at the Beginning of
Becoming . . . with God!

When The Pain Is Severe

It was my high school pal.

She had gone to a state university. She was given the
job of editor of the newspaper. She had been euphoric in
her plans to make it the best in the nation. All summer she
had stayed on campus working night and day on her
dream.

School opened. Her first prized edition was released.
She sighed with joyful relief and sat back to await the
response.

It came.

But it wasn't what she had expected.

Instead of being hailed as a budding William Allen
White, she was called "traitor," "irresponsible," "com-
munist," and other unexpected, unwanted epithets.
Stunned, she could hardly believe what was happening.

In the second issue, she wrote an editorial trying to

52

articulate her dreams for the paper and what she had hoped to accomplish.

After its release, she was called into the office and summarily fired.

She called and asked me to meet her at the airport. She was flying across country to be with me.

She couldn't wait to talk, so we went into the airport restaurant where she could pour out all of her pain. I had never seen such raw human suffering as lay in her eyes. They were like twin martyr fires smouldering in a crushed and torn spirit that throbbed like a puppy overrun on the highway . . . ready to die.

This kind of suffering demanded more than pat answers, memorized Scripture, pious clichés. I could only give her the gifts of my sharing and caring.

Later, back at the dorm as we lay in the darkness that night, she brought up the subject of meaning . . . or meaninglessness . . . and then she said something that made me sit up.

Being a journalist, she spoke with clarity. She said: "Everyone seems to be staring, glaring, rushing, screaming, forgetting life . . . forgetting love . . . forgetting about being real people."

She sighed. "All honesty has gone under. . . drowned in the war we lost!"

That is what caught me.

"What war did we lose?"

"The war to wrest meaning out of human existence." She sat up. "What I've been telling you, Ruth, is that disillusionment is here. Sartre, Camus are right. Life is absurd!"

I jumped up and turned on the light. I went to my desk

and leafed through my notebook. I found a paper I had written after my first exposure to Sartre and Camus. In preparing for it, I had made a list of quotes I found interesting.

I took the sheet from the folder and handed it to her. "You might find this dialogue stimulating."

She took it and began to read:

What else is there to make life tolerable? We stand on the shore of an ocean, crying to the night and the emptiness; sometimes a voice answers out of the darkness. But it is the voice of one drowning; and in a moment a silence returns. The world seems to me quite dreadful; the unhappiness of many people is very great, and I often wonder how they endure it. To know people is to know their tragedy; it is usually the central thing about which their lives are built. And I suppose if they did not live most of the time in the things of the moment, they would not be able to go on.

—BERTRAND RUSSELL

She looked up in appreciation. She had found a kindred spirit. "He says it so well," she said softly.

Her eyes returned to the page.

I've been a failure. I've had a wretched life. And I've made a hash of everything.

—SOMERSET MAUGHAM

Death—not sex—is the basic cause of man's psychic disorders. The clamor of sex drowns out the ever-waiting presence of death ... death is the symbol of ultimate impotence and finiteness. What would we see if we cut through our obsession with sex? That we must die.

—DR. ROLLO MAY, PSYCHOANALYST

54

We live in a vacuum. The frustration of an urban society, the emptiness of materialism press in on us. We children of technology sing hollow-eyed in the face of absolute annihilation, empty outlines eaten by an inner intensity we can't name; our elusive dreams evaporate as we lunge at them.
—J. FITZGERALD, COLLEGE STUDENT

She was smiling. "They understand," she said. "How sad for them . . . for me . . . and, in spite of your faith, someday for you . . . but this is reality."
She returned to the typed quotes. There was only one more.

Whosoever will save his life shall lose it; but whosoever shall lose his life for my sake . . . shall save it . . . Come unto me, all ye that labor and are heavy laden, and I will give you rest . . . [I have] come to save that which was lost . . . [I did not come] to be ministered unto, but to minister and to give [my] life a ransom for many . . . He that doeth truth cometh to the light . . . I am the light of the world: he who followeth me shall not walk in darkness, but shall have the light of life . . . If any man thirst, let him come unto me and drink . . . the Father which sent me, he gave me a commandment, what I should say, and what I should speak. And I know that his commandment is life everlasting . . . Heaven and earth shall pass away: but my words shall not pass away.*

—HISTORY'S GREATEST REVOLUTIONARY
JESUS OF NAZARETH

She didn't look up. She just sat with her head down, her eyes searching the words. I had no idea what she was

*Mark 8:35; Matt. 11:28; Matt. 18:11; Matt. 20:28; John 3:21; John 8:12; John 7:37; John 12: 49,50; Luke 21:33.

thinking. I didn't know what communication she was receiving. It had been my best inspiration to confront her with Personality.

When she spoke her voice was husky. She read the last line on the page: "Heaven and earth shall pass away: but my words shall not pass away."

Her breath shuddered.

"How I long for that kind of security! In a topsy-turvy world where everything has been blasted to bits for me, how I yearn for unchangingness."

She looked at me then.

"You've been with this Jesus for a long time now. Do you *really* find all of this to be true?"

"Every word."

"But you've had pain in your life. I know about some keen disappointments . . . I know about your mother's illness . . . I know about your brother's suffering . . . Have you really found Him to be a light in the midst of *all* that dark?"

"Every time."

"Like Bertrand Russell, I stand in the darkness alone . . . but here is a Voice promising light and His presence. Now. Forever."

Out of my own experience, I could assert with the psalmist: "When the pain is severe, He is near to comfort."

"You've proven that to be fact?" Her eyes searched me out.

I could only smile in the certainty of it. "I've proven that to be fact."

We sat together, in the small dormitory room, lost in the awesome wonder that "When the pain is severe, He will be near to comfort . . ."

We both knew that that reality would make all the

difference in every facet of our future lives as we poised at the Beginning of Becoming . . . with God!

ℋe Is Near To Comfort

It was her crossroads.

The past and the future were fused in the excruciating pain of her broken present. Whatever choice she made, life would never be the same for her again.

Bertrand Russell invited her to walk in darkness.

Jesus Christ challenged: "T U
R
N with Me.
"I know new roads that lead
to new worlds
That will be best for the
uniqueness of you
If you dare
to follow Me."

And He had promised: "I am the light of the world: he who followeth me shall not walk in darkness, but shall have the light of life."*

Darkness/Light.

She had to choose.

Alone.

*John 8:12

After awhile, she put the paper away. I turned off the lamp and we lay back in our beds.

I finally slept, releasing her to the privacy of her cross-roads stance.

She tells me she did not sleep.

She considered . . .

she debated. . .

she fought . . .

she cried . . .

and somewhere, in the long hours, she turned the lamp back on and wrote this poem to God.

Dear Sir:

I address you formally
Because I do not know You well.
In fact, as we both know,
Until tonight I did not know You
At all.

Like Russell before me,
I stand on the shore of an ocean,
Crying to the night and the emptiness;
Only the Voice I hear
Is not of one drowning
But of One proclaiming
"I am the Light of the World."

In the night of my blackness,
In the emptiness of broken self-made goals,
I would be foolish not to
Rush to the Voice of Light
Asking that You dispel the Dark

58

With the floodlight
Of Your sun.

Now I pause in embarrassment.
I have no right to such petition.
I bow my head
And try again.

Dear Sir:

I am in pain.
Will You comfort me?
I am in darkness.
Will you guide me?
I am dependent.
Will You, the Light of the World,
Take my hand?
I will follow
One step at a time
Believing that one day
I shall not walk in darkness
But shall, indeed, have
Your promised Light of life.

And Sir:

Thank You.
Very much.

Many years later, she now paces through an important life steeped in sun-glow. But she walks on a foundation formed in the crucible of stark suffering. Her life is

now completely God-directed because, in deep darkness, she found the Light of life . . .

In that small dormitory room, she discovered for herself that "When the pain is severe, He is near to comfort" and that knowledge changed everything, as she poised at the Beginning of Becoming . . . with God!

———————— ❧ ————————

When The Burden Is Heavy

It was my endurance-peak.

I sagged with weariness. Every corpuscle screamed for rest. Every muscle rebelled with fury.

Still I plodded one foot in front of the other.

Classes.

Committees.

Plays.

Performances.

Grades.

Goals.

People.

Pressures.

Duties.

Demands.

It was a ceaseless treadmill.

And I, ever straining for perfection, was so *tired*!

One morning, I trudged to the post office between classes to pick up my mail. There was a letter from my father.

I went to the doughnut shop down the street to read it. I tore open the envelope and grinned at the beloved stilted opening:

"Dearest Ruth:

Greetings in Jesus' Name."

He began every letter like that. I supposed it was appropriate when he wrote the church's general superintendent or when he wrote his annual report to the local church board. But here to his youngest child, he formally began as if writing a profound epistle.

Instead of profundity, he informed me about the status of his garden, the attendance of the Sunday school, and the recent repairs on his car. He told me about my mother's physical condition, and his learning how to do the housework. Then he was ready to conclude.

Just as his letter-salutations were the same, so were his letter-conclusions. He was always admonishing me about trying to do too much. As I smiled at his openings, so I smiled at his endings and let them go on by me without a second thought.

But this time he caught my attention.

"I know you'll be good to others," he wrote. "I'm asking you to be good to yourself. Remember: Too much of 'this and that' can lead to personal impoverishment."

I re-read that paragraph and let my eyes finish the page: "I know you'll be good to others. I'm asking you to be good to yourself. Remember: Too much of 'this and that' can lead to personal impoverishment.

Love and prayers,

Daddy."

My eyes blurred with tears as I focused on the spidery signature.

In the booth, I whispered the words:
Love and prayers,
Daddy.

How warm I felt to be blanketed in the love and prayers of this beautiful man who was my daddy. Taking time from his much-loved sermon preparation, he had sat at the big upright manual typewriter and, with two fingers, had "greeted" me in "Jesus' Name," pounded out a report of activities, and concluded with an admonishment sent with his love and prayers.

I looked at my watch.

Time for class.

But I didn't want to go today. I was tired.

I wanted to take a walk, stop the clock, simply stalk
a thought or two
a personal view
of my own.

I *should* go to class . . . but maybe not . . . My eyes went back to the letter.

I laughed and went to the cash register. I paid for the doughnut and asked the girl if I could leave my books with her. I had something to attend to. She smilingly took the load and put them on an inside bench. She wished me a good day and I thanked her, sincerely.

There was a bounce in my step as I went through the door and down the street for the rural roads I loved so well. When I knew I was completely alone in the secluded land, I began to run.

I ran and ran until I fell underneath a tree breathless,
perspiring,
laughing.

I looked about and when I could speak I proclaimed to all listening birds and squirrels:

"I hold the right to snatch some moments
Only God and I can share. . .
Unjudged, unmeasured, unexplained
Joyful, expansive, moments of the spirit
When I can pause to clap my hands
And shout with God:
This is life!
Enjoy!"

It was a moment I shall always remember with delight.

It was a moment when I learned that "When the burden is heavy" I need to get away from partitioned life and be with Him who "is there to lean upon."

Not to do so leads to "personal impoverishment."

To do so leads to "His Sufficiency" for all my needs.

I need to internalize that truth now . . . even as I initially did when I poised at the Beginning of Becoming . . . with God!

He Is There To Lean Upon

It was the night before final exams.

The burden was heavy, and there was no time to break away for relief in schedule-shattering moments of focus-change.

The only way I would make it with desired grades through this semester was to remain true to the clock, rooted in the grind, faithful to the task.

But the burden *was* heavy.

I had been working extra hours at my job. A strongly disciplined student, I usually had my term work done prior to its due-date. That had proven impossible.

So I had been working hour-after-hour-after-hour on semester-due papers, projects, and reports. Completely exhausted, I now stared at a pile of books over which I would have three final exams the next day.

One of my friends had already bid me goodnight. She was going to bed with a debonair heart.

"I will ask God to help me with the tests," she said.

And she believed He would.

I wistfully looked at my bed. But I didn't move from the chair. I believed I could not ask for God's help on the tests unless the request was *just* . . . and it could not be *just* unless I had done my best in diligent study.

So sighing deeply, I pulled the top book in front of me and opened its pages. I worked through discussions about DNA, cytoplasm, neurons.

My mind followed the word-guide through respiration, replication, photosynthesis.

Then I pulled down the second book. It was biology and I perused information about amoebae, paramecia algae . . . and then I sagged.

My eyes burned.

My stomach churned.

My mind moved with the alacrity

of a fly caught in molasses.

I got up and walked about the room.

I stopped at the window and knelt before it, leaning my head against the cold glass.

"I'm so tired," I whispered.

"I know," He said.

I grinned.

"I cannot do this unless Thou enablest me," I quoted.

"I know," He said.

I sobered.

"Even with all this study, my mind may be so tired that I will forget it all." I worried.

"Your helplessness leads you to My sufficiency," He said.

I looked up at His stars twinkling on the velvety canopy of sky.

"There are two of us involved in this, right?

God, the Creator

I, the created."

"I will not leave you," He said.

"Even when I should have gone to work earlier? Even when I should have studied sooner? Even when I'm so tired I think I'll drop?"

His smile was deep in love and I cuddled in its security as He said: "Even when!"

Refreshed by His steadfast assurance, I went back to the desk and dragged open the third book. My slow-moving brain explored facts about Caruso, Munsel, Callas . . .

My memory-cells received documentation about Gershwin, Bach, Tchaikovsky . . .

And then, having done my best, I closed the book, prayed the prayer that I considered just, and went to bed.

The next morning my hand swiftly moved filling in the blanks on the dittoed pages . . . I paused to ruffle through the test . . . It seemed the blanks on the pages were interminable.

The burden is heavy, my heart whispered.

"Peace I leave with you," He whispered inside, "my

peace I give unto you . . . Let not your heart be troubled, neither let it be afraid."*

I leaned hard in the comfort of His love and then I turned back and began filling in the blanks.

Final exams are no longer my burden. But the heaviness of the loads I am asked to bear seems to increase in crushing weight each year. Sometimes I break away for respite, sometimes I keep plodding on, but always I depend on the *fact* that "when the burden is heavy, He is there to lean upon. . ."

What a glorious knowledge to gain at the early moments of my Beginning of Becoming . . . with God!

*John 14:27

When Depression Darkens My Soul

It was like I was in a box. I couldn't breathe; I couldn't move; I couldn't even think. Nothing was going right; no big problem; just little things about everything. Dusty. Drab. Daily. Dreary. Depression mushroomed until it enshrouded every facet of every day. It was like I was in a box.

It was a mountain of collected small things. My brother didn't write. . .

66

My roommate borrowed my red dress and spilled unwashable ink on its skirt. . .

A library book had been misplaced and the fine hung over me. . .

An unexpected emergency at work meant missing a much-longed-for concert date. . .

Two of my friends were fighting. . .

My driver's license had expired. . .

Landslide of catastrophe!

> Self-pity crushed me in a box. My brother must not love me anymore. I would never be able to find a dress as attractive as the red full-skirted faille one. The library fine would wipe out my chances for a new pair of shoes. I never had any fun. I never had a moment of peace. I was discriminated against . . . woe! Woe was mine. Self-pity crushed me in a box.

I lived in the depression for days.

Cramped, crushed, cringed . . . tightly fitted in the box of despair . . . unadmittedly unwilling for release . . . righteously reveling in the suffocation of self-pity.

I closed my eyes in the soul-darkness.

Disillusionment flooded over me.

I was besieged in the thickets of my night.

There were confused alarms, ignorant armies, clashes of blood and sinew.

> Depression clutched
> my life in its talon

grip and the only
sound was a mourn-
ful dirge I sang. I was
in a box.

And there I remained, mesmerized with the rhythm of
my own pain, the best of my funeral music in minor key.
It was my choice.

And I could be there yet.

My Constant Companion respects my free will so
profoundly that He would not pull me out of the box until I
asked.

I finally wearied of the self-torture, and I hushed the
wailing dirge of self-pity and whispered: "Are You there?"

"I will never leave you," was the prompt response . . .
from outside the box, where He was patiently waiting
where I had left Him.

"Is there a way out of this thing?" I asked, ashamed.

I could feel His amusement. "Knock and it shall be
opened,"* He said.

Abashed, I weakly lifted a cramped hand and
knocked . . . The boundaries of the box dissolved, the
dank atmosphere was purged with cascades of fresh air,
the constrictions relaxed and my muscles luxuriously expanded . . .

I stood and stretched.

The tensions flowed out like water from a drip-dry
garment.

The ever-pressing weight of depression slid off my
backbone.

The box was gone and I was free.

I grinned ruefully.

"My father said: 'When you are afraid of a thing, you

*Matt. 7:7

68

are basically in doubt about God's interest in it with you . . . and that's unfair . . . to you and to Him.' " I ran my fingers through my hair. "I guess I forgot."

His quietness throbbed with loving understanding.

"I'll probably forget again," I admitted. "I'll let fear mash me back into the confines of depression's dark box. Please stay with me," I pleaded. "Even though I'm unfair to You by submitting to that dark depressive box."

"Even though," He said.

And so I have His promise.

When depression darkens my soul . . . contorts me in a box . . . He will stay with me . . . and when I knock, He will open the binding structure and touch me with eternal joy! No matter how many things go wrong, I have no need to fear for . . . there are always two of us involved:

God, the Creator

I, the created.

I had found a major foundation-stone for life as I poised at the Beginning of Becoming . . . with God!

He Touches Me With Eternal Joy

It was my dizzying moment of exultation!

Freed from demands and pressures for an entire day, I had taken notebook and pen to my favorite wooded area outside of town. Hour after hour, my fingers would unreel the coils of my adventure with God.

On that yellow pad, I set down this account of divine touch with eternal joy:

> My throat aches.
>
> My heart hurts with song as I pause under the sapphire sky of summer morning and witness the majestic beauty of my world.
>
> The mischievous breeze trips by, her silvery green garments caressing each flower, each weed, each tree; the transparent brook is hushed by the advent of the golden dawn so that the fragrant air holds no sounds of her ripples, her dances, her music. The saucy robin hops about in sheer delight, filled with a happy flame, and the lilac-laden air intoxicates my being.
>
> In the blue tide of a dawning summer morning, I feel that I could touch infinity as I listen to nature's symphony to God!
>
> My soul is aflame.
>
> My thoughts thrill in gratitude as I stand in the summer noontime in the midst of a berry patch and lend my inner eyes to the view of the multicolored tapestry of my world.
>
> The cottontail hiding here in sequestered thickets, alarmed at the tinkle of my laugh, bounds away in a flurry of dust and fur; the cocky jay sits in the oak tree protesting my presence and scolding my awkward movements; the pheasant in the willows waves his brilliant plumage like a glorious scarf of wind. The gaily singing brook looks up through tall, leaning grass and reflects the majesty of heaven in its claret

cup. In the hot enchantment of summer, I sail blithely outward to sunlit ports as I listen to nature's symphony to God!

My spirit is at peace.

My yearnings find fulfillment as the plum-colored dusk drowns the pumpkin-yellow sun and dancing breezes fill the air with gentleness and rest. I stand with my back to a persimmon tree in summer twilight, resting my head in the leaf shadow's soft depth of sapphire, and listen to a wood thrush twirling music like a band of gold in which to rest my spirit. The little brook pulls up blankets of shadowed light and sings a medley of soft lullabies to the newborn bluebirds in the tall oak trees. The deep-blue darkness flows into the night and here, in the crispness of summer evening, I am sandaled with love and with rest; my being is caressed with wind and with moonglow, and I thrill to the sounds of the combined musicians about me rendering in unparalleled splendor the majesty of nature's symphony to God!

For an entire golden day I allowed my heart to bask in joy. Too often allowing worries, disappointments, duties to cobweb happiness into stillness, I tossed everything aside and allowed the full focus of my attentions to spotlight wonder. I spent hour after hour consciously reveling in God's world, God's presence, God's love, God's course designed for the uniqueness of me . . .

unreeled in the past . . .

now visible in the present . . .

promised for the future . . .

Life, I was learning, is a carousel of changing seasons.

In the whirling dervish of activity, it is easy to bypass the season of pure joy.

We dream. . .

We dare. . .

We purpose. . .

We perform. . . and when pain comes, we take time
to cry. . .

when fatigue comes, we take
time to gasp. . .

when depression comes, we
take time to ache. . .

but too often when good things crown our lives, we assume them as our natural rights and race on, never taking time to *revel* in God's joy.

And that omission is "personal impoverishment" and should be shunned.

Since that long-ago day when I penned my description of the way God "touches me with eternal joy" through the beauty of His world, I have tried to incorporate a mental search for such seasons.

Sometimes they come in periods when I am free to fully explore each dimension of the joy and even set it down in words . . . even more frequently they come in small moments clutched on the carousel; as I spin through busy activities, I mentally focus on how *happy* I am to be here . . . listening to *this* music . . . a part of the multicolored throbbing vitality of my orbit . . . and sometimes they come in periods when depression has me in its grip and I, by an act of will, strain even a finger through the iron jaws of unpleasant circumstances and ask God to touch me with His eternal joy . . . and I have found that no matter how dark the box of life-less-than-ideal,

He always helps me discover elements that *are* ideal, people who *are* noble, life-gifts that *are* pure gold.

In such discovery, He gave the power to dispel dreariness.

In such discovery,
> "When depression darkens my soul,
> He touches me with eternal joy."

That is a forever-truth . . . for me then
for me now
for you as you poise at the
Beginning of Becoming . . . with God!

When I Feel Empty And Alone

It was J.

He was a senior when I was a freshman in high school. I was stunningly impressed with his ability to debate. When he came to my house with his freshman-cousin one night, I listened wide-eyed to his eloquent rhetoric. I was certain that all of his views were knowledgeable and profound.

Because I was such an eager listener, we became friends. Although we never dated, we spent a lot of time over malteds in the drug store: he expounding; I absorbing.

He went to college.

When he returned on vacation, we were both surprised to observe that I had learned how to talk. My parents, teachers, and peers had always been cognizant of that fact. But my relationship with J had been totally in the role of listener.

As he had matured that year at college, so, we found, had I. So instead of monologues over malteds, we began debates. It was great fun. But after that vacation, our paths went totally separate ways.

I sent him a graduation announcement at the time of my triumph over high school. As a gift, he sent me a neatly typed copy of his philosophy of life. That was my first exposure to the word "existentialism," which he defined "as nothing else than an attempt to draw all the consequences of a coherent atheistic position."

That was the first time I knew he no longer believed in God.

After arriving at college, I was exposed to Jean-Paul Sartre and learned that he, who had given J's definition of existentialism to the world, believed that man is alone, living in a universe without values and without meaning. Man is alone to create his own values and his own destiny. "Man is nothing else but what he makes of himself."

I could not accept it.

It made no sense to me.

So when I was assigned to write a paper on my philosophy of life, I attempted to discredit his thesis. I smile now at the effort. I was eighteen, unlearned, uneloquent, unsophisticated, armed with the goal of refuting the razor-sharp mind of a world-renowned French philosopher.

I sent J a copy of the paper.

He called me.

"I got your essay," he told me. "What makes you so sure you aren't just whistling in the dark?"

"Reality," I answered.

He didn't respond.

I was surprised. J always had a free-wheeling answer for everything.

As the silence expanded, I became uneasy.

"Deep inside, no matter how intense my desires, I would *know* if I were alone whistling in the dark! I'm not just articulating theory. I have *experientially* proven that I face life with Someone. There are always two of us involved:

    God, the Creator

    I, the created."

There was more silence.

When he spoke, his usual mercurial voice jerked with pain.

"Your paper came at a bad time," he confessed. "I can usually face the absurdity of life with bravado. I can assert that I will die like an animal with a laugh. I can talk about emptiness and keep going. Usually. Today I can't. Problems have been complicating my life until the loneliness has become more acute than I think I can bear. And then, in the mail, comes this young girl's proclamation that she lives in 'constant companionship'; there is 'divine design in our lives that is ongoing through this world and into the next; our God-dreams become realities as we walk through life with Him.'"

The silence returned.

"I don't want to change my mind," he said huskily into the phone, "just because I feel so beaten, so alien, so terribly lonely."

"Why?" I asked. "What better reason could there be?

You've tried your philosophy and found it too bitter to bear."

The silence echoed between us again. I knew I could not argue brilliantly. I also sensed that argument was not the point. Ultimately, one's "philosophy of life" has to be chosen out of more than intellectual gymnastics. It has to square with all of life.

J began reading. The quote was from John Oxenham.

> To every man there openeth
> A Way, and Ways, and a Way,
> And the High Soul climbs the High Way,
> And the Low Soul gropes the Low,
> And in between on the misty flats,
> The rest drift to and fro.
> But to every man there openeth
> A High Way and a Low,
> And every man decideth
> The Way his soul shall go.

I felt his pain throbbing across the wires.

"I desperately want to be honest," he cried. "One part of my mind says that what I read is just a poet's thoughts . . . it isn't necessarily truth . . . and yet posited before me in your paper I find a polarity of chosen life-ways. Yours couldn't be more opposite from mine.

"And from the aching vacuum of my emptiness and loneliness, it seems I have to believe that the 'High Way' would be a 'Companioned Way.' The High Way would be one with 'Divine Design.' The High Way would be a walk with God the Creator. Surely that is higher than laboring under the burden that man is totally alone; man is only

76

what he makes of himself; and after death, man is annihi-
lated like an animal run down in the street.

"But I'm reasoning from the desperation of my
feelings of alienation. Perhaps I cannot be reasonable
now . . ."

"Perhaps you are most reasonable now," I
suggested. "Perhaps it is only when we come to the final
end of human sufficiency that we have to reach out for
divine help. Fulton Oursler assumed the atheistic position
in his adult life. Ultimately trouble flooded his life until he
felt frantic for a Power higher than his own. But he had
never believed in God. He could not pretend now out of
need. He did admit that he *wished* he could believe."

"Oh I *wish* that with all my heart," J sighed. "What
became of his wish?"

"He decided that faith is a gift. And if a gift, it can be
asked for. Remembering the man in the Bible who prayed:
"Lord, I believe; help thou mine unbelief,"* he decided to
bow in a church on Fifth Avenue one blustery afternoon.
There, he asked for faith. And then he said to God:

> In ten minutes or less I may change my mind . . . I may scoff
> at all this—and love error again. Pay no attention to me
> then. For this little time I am in my right mind and heart.
> This is my best. Take it and forget the rest; and, if You are
> really there, help me.**

"He must have felt a lot like I feel," J mused. "I have
felt such an urge to pray since I read your paper . . . but I
held back knowing that if and when my problems are

*Mark 9:24

**Fulton Oursler, *Why I Know There Is a God* (New York: Double-
day, 1950), p. 20.

77

ironed out, I might hate myself for my weakness . . ."

" 'And love error again?' " I quoted from Oursler. "He felt that only in his stark human need had he finally come to his 'right mind and heart' . . . his 'best.' Perhaps that is true of us all. We can strut about parroting that 'man is what he makes of himself' until life slaps us into the whirlwind of our own weaknesses and we know that all is lost unless there is Someone stronger and wiser than we."

"God, I have never believed in You. You know all about that."

In awe, I realized that I was sharing a holy moment via long distance telephone.

"But I am empty and alone and helpless. I need You to be real. Help Thou my unbelief."

There was no thunder or lightning.

But a warm hush pervaded both our spirits. Silence again vibrated on the wires. Finally J said: "I have a lot to work out. I'll keep in touch."

Through all the intervening years, he has illuminated my life with reports of the excitement of his God-ventures in a world of "divine design" where he has "constant-companionship."

The psalmist wrote centuries ago: "When I feel empty and alone He fills the aching vacuum with His power."

The intellectual young J found it true in modern times during a telephone conversation with a friend. He has proven its reality through many years of personal experience with God as his Constant Companion.

There are always two involved in each facet of life: God, the Creator
    I, the created.

In that knowledge, one can dynamically, confidently, securely poise at the Beginning of Becoming . . . with God!

He Fills The Aching Vacuum With His Power

It was J's new philosophy of life.

He sent it bound and neatly typed to companion the original. "The Revised Version," he called it. It truly was a contrast.

Here are parts of it.

I have always admired adventurers. My hero was Admiral Richard E. Byrd. I can recount his exploits in detail. That I never considered the motivating philosophy of his life now amazes me. But I did not. He was a Wonder-Man, set apart from mere mortals. His arena was exterior achievement. I never contemplated his interior thoughts. Thus it was a shock when I finally was confronted with this aspect of his writings. The following especially captured my attention:

The day was dying, the night was being born—but with great peace. Here were the imponderable processes and forces of the cosmos, harmonious and soundless. Harmony, that was it! That was what came out of the silence—a gentle rhythm, the strain of a perfect chord, the music of the spheres, perhaps. It was enough to catch that rhythm, momentarily to be myself a part of it. In that instant

I could feel no doubt of man's oneness with the universe. The conviction came that that rhythm was too orderly, too harmonious, too perfect to be a product of blind chance— that, therefore, there must be purpose in the whole and that man was part of that whole and not an accidental offshoot. It was a feeling that transcended reason; that went to the heart of man's despair and found it groundless. The universe was a cosmos, not a chaos; man was as rightfully a part of that cosmos as were the day and night.*

I have never stood at the South Pole as a conquering adventurer. But I have stood alone in the night as the conviction mushroomed through my being that there must be purpose in the whole and that man was part of that whole and not an accidental offshoot. It was a feeling that transcended reason; that went to the heart of [my] despair and found it groundless. And in that discovery came such a change in my being that the need for this revised paper was born.

J proceeded, from that introduction, into a detailing of his previous philosophy and the empty, lonely, aching vacuum into which it had thrust him. He had known himself helpless in the vacuum and since he had conceded no assistance outside himself, he had longed for death. Even annihilation, he had felt, "would be superior to never-ending grief."

In the midst of this depression came his confrontation with the quote from Oxenham and my own triumphant testimony. He set down the account of our telephone conversation and the quoted words of Oursler: "For this little time I am in my right mind and heart. This is my best." And then he cited the thought of Lin Yutang:

*Source unknown.

80

This is the stupendous fact about man and his spiritual striving after God. It is not faith; it is not a contradiction of reason; it is merely a healthy instinct. It is man's total response to the universe through his moral nature. It is not the antithesis of reason; it is the higher reason.

J proceeded to explore the "higher reason" of opening one's spirit to God. He related what had happened to him.

After I hung up the telephone, I sat on the floor with the instrument still in my lap. The seething fury of my soul had slowly calmed into immobility and it seemed as if I were merely waiting. For what, I knew not. But there was no strain. There was no impatience. I did not move.

And then an emotion never experienced before swept down upon me. I said aloud: 'Lord God, I give you my will.' I was surprised, for I had not ever considered giving God my will. My concern had been in His existence. Now suddenly I felt propelled into a new realm of life and my immediate response by-passed the question of divine existence and concluded something dynamically viable: surrender of my will to Another.

It may be, I reasoned, that the created inwardly knows of its Creator in spite of all garnered doubts. In the inner core of my being, that fact may have always been acknowledged. Therefore, when I actually sat in His Presence, it was predictable that the inner "I" would move on to something that had not yet been settled, but which I wanted to settle very much.

I know about life under my own will. It is empty,

chaotic, meaningless. I am now ready to walk the High Way following another Will. I have proved my own insufficient. I am now ready to prove His. I choose to make God my leader.

His final sentences were:

> In my previous paper, I began my last paragraph thus: "We live in a vacuum." I was speaking from experience. I was trapped in a vacuum in which there was "emptiness," "hollow-eyes," and "elusive dreams" that "evaporate as we lunge at them." I am convinced this vacuum existence is the ultimate in agony. The atmosphere of despair is so heavy one slowly suffocates into oblivion.
>
> To conclude this paper, I shall repeat a friend who paraphrased my original thus: "We live in constant companionship." As she spoke from experience, so now I speak from the same experience. I now abide in a "constant companionship" in which there is fulfillment, purposeful-eyes, and "God-dreams" that "become realities" in exciting, astonishing, supernatural ways. I am convinced that this "constant companionship" is the ultimate in human joy. The atmosphere of divine love is so exhilarating one walks with radiance in this world and into the next.

The psalmist summarized J's "Revised Version" in one glorious sentence in Psalm 23: "When I feel empty and alone He fills the aching vacuum with His power."

What joy to stand secure at the Beginning of Becoming . . . with God!

My Security Is In His Promise

It was my anxiety.

I could tell from my parents' letters that doctor bills and medicine expenses were rising constantly higher. The strain of their continuing to support me seemed to be at the breaking point. I was working as many hours at my secretarial job as I could, but it was never enough for all expenses.

What would I do if I had to quit using their checking account?

What would I do if I lost my job?

What would I do if I lost my scholarship for the next semester?

My hands knotted in fear . . .

My stomach churned in agitation . . .

My mind raced with the dreadful possibilities . . .

What if . . .

What if . . .

What if . . .

and then, for a moment, logic captured the winging bat of fear . . .

My father was an amazing financier. He had succeeded in supporting seven other children into maturity . . . Would he not, just as skillfully, find a way with the eighth?

My boss had introduced me to her brother only the week before with the words: "She is total efficiency." Did that sound like I was being prepared to lose my job?

The scholarship was for four years with the only stipulation a required gradepoint. Since that had never been a problem, why should the scholarship be considered in jeopardy?

But the bat of fear broke away from logic and zoomed back into my spirit.

There was always the possibility that events would occur so that I would be totally stranded financially. What would I *do*?

Then I remembered a line I had memorized from the writings of E. Stanley Jones. He had said that worriers "smother themselves, for it is not the native air we should breathe. Faith, not worry, is our native air."

I remembered that my parents had always seemed to abide in that "native air" of faith. They had believed unshakably the promise: "Seek ye first the kingdom of God and his righteousness and *all these things* shall be added unto you."* And . . . as I could see in the lives of my siblings and in the lives of my parents to this point . . . *all these things* . . . such as food, clothing, books, education, doctors, medicine . . . had been added in full measure.

"Faith is our native air." Abiding in that climate of active, unswerving faith had enabled my parents to face life in all its changing seasons with eight children, to move on the basis of things hoped for, on the foundation of things unseen.

My mind went back to a day in high school when, in teen-age grief over a personal loss, I had run to my favorite oak tree. My mother had followed behind, and after plac-

*Matt. 6:33, italics added.

84

ing her hand on my heaving shoulder, she had said: "Honey, don't cry. Look about you. See the lovely gracefulness of the fern bathing in the shower of sunlight. Hear the gossamer lyrics from the bees, the wind crooning in the treetops. Beauty is here. But look, you see both life and death. Here is a green leaf: alive and swaying. Here is a brown leaf: dead and fallen. The lesson you must learn today is that everything you can *see* will perish. When you need a foundation for life, something strong to which you can always cling—it must be *unseen*.

"You must have the consciousness within you deep and true that there is a God, that God loves you, that you are in His hands. And then, whether life or death, joy or sorrow, all is well. You can only trust in that which you cannot see. These tangible things will pass away. But your intangible faith will support you through every storm. You will walk on what is seemingly void, but you will always find the unseen Rock beneath."

I realized that the fears I had were rooted in some basis. The financial details of my college education were not as well-defined as Jeanie's whose trust fund, established at her birth, held more than enough for college and graduate school if she desired. But to focus on my fears was unfair, to me and to God. For, as my father had said that long-ago crossroads-day, "Whenever you are afraid of a thing, you are basically in doubt about God's interest in it with you." No, my financial sufficiency could not be *seen* in a bank balance. But it was assured in the *unseen* fact that there were two of us involved: God, the Creator I, the created.

Now, years later, I look back on God's supplying *all my needs* for not only that college degree, but later for the

M.A. and the Ph.D. Oh yes, my heart now exults: "Seek ye first the kingdom of God and his righteousness and *all these things* shall be added unto you!"

The psalmist David rejoiced: "My security is in His promise," and he and I offer that security to you with assurance.
Claim it.
Believe it.
Trust in it.
You are secure in His promise as you poise at the Beginning of Becoming . . . with God!

To Be Near Me Always

It was my first life-hurricane.
I had faced life-showers of disappointment.
I had faced life-hail, which had shattered dreams.
I had faced life-storms where darkness engulfed and plans were blown out of sight.
But this was different.
I faced disillusionment on an untried level. I faced criticism of an unknown degree. I faced a life-hurricane that threatened to leave me devastated.
But as I poised at the Beginning of Becoming . . . I found that "my security is in His promise to be near me always. . . ." and victory was mine.
Later, I wrote about the experience in these words:

86

The thunder crashed!
The lightning rolled!
The world was cold and fierce!

I looked about and there were only the wailing wind and the naked trees. The dead leaves blew in whispering swirls about my feet. The rain knifed down relentlessly. The storm raged fierce and wild.

And I stood in the midst of the storm—frightened, bewildered, and aching with pain. Those in whom I had trusted had turned away, indifferent to my plight. Those on whom I had leaned had backed away, leaving me to stand alone in the midst of the fury. Those with whom I had laughed and played had only a glance of pity and had turned a deaf ear to my cry.

I stood alone!

I shouted, but the sound was lost in the midst of the pounding storm. I groaned, but its echo bounced against the stony heavens. I wept, but the salty tears only made rivulets down my frightened face. In the midst of turmoil, with all friends gone away, I stood alone.

And then—suddenly—I wasn't alone! For Someone was there beside me. He had a strong voice and the sound of His voice calmed the storm. The thunder quieted. The lightning ceased. The wind hushed to an anthem. And this is what He spoke to me: "I, the Lord, am your Shepherd: even though you walk through the valley of the shadow of death, you need never fear, for I am with you."

And in that moment my pain was healed, for I realized that those who had turned away, those whose opinions I had valued so much, those who had wounded so mercilessly, were not important after all. For I was serving a higher authority, a higher purpose, a higher commission. The Lord was with me! That was all that mattered!

This beloved Twenty-third Psalm, which came to me in that moment of crisis, best expresses my relationship with God. I have faced life in all of its changing seasons. I have found, as others have, that it is easy to serve and trust Him when the sky is sapphire and the sun casts about us its shafts of golden light, but it is not so easy when the sky is leaden and the storm crashes in.

But I have learned the glorious truth that, through His grace, I *can* surmount the storm! Through His power, I *can* overcome the pain! Through His strength, I *can* serve Him even under tremendous pressure!

With the presence of the Shepherd close by, I can be triumphant . . . *no matter the weather!*

It is truth: in sun, in rain
in calm, in storm
in light, in dark
[Your] Security is in His promise
to be near [you] always . . .
Build your life-foundation on that as you poise at the Beginning of Becoming . . . with God!

---　❧　---

And In The Knowledge

It was a life-molding fact.

I wrote it in my diary.

As I concluded the thought, I sat staring at the words. Somehow I had internalized it. This was my first confrontation with it consciously.

Surprised at my own understanding, I re-read the entry:

"There are two doors to knowledge of God: the intellectual, the experiential.

The former is important; the latter is vital."

I had spent the day in skull-busting study for a paper in a religion class. I had carefully researched the arguments for proving God intellectually.

I had considered the fact that whatever is in motion must be moved by another, for motion is the response of matter to power. In the world of matter, there can be no power without life, and life presupposes a being from which emanates the power to move things such as the tides and the planets.

I had perused the argument that says nothing can be the cause of itself. It would be prior to itself if it caused itself to be, and that is an absurdity.

89

I had explored the argument from the laws of the universe. We see objects that have no intellect, such as stars and planets, moving and rotating in a consistent pattern, cooperating ingeniously with one another. It is evident that they achieve their movements not by accident but by design. Whatever lacks intelligence cannot of itself move intelligently. A bow and arrow would be useless without an archer. What gives direction and purpose and design to our environment if not a Creator-Being?

And then, after setting down valid intellectual knowledge, I wrote in my diary: "There are two doors to knowledge of God: the intellectual,
> the experiential.
>> The former is important; the latter is vital."

I looked at the words carefully.

At that moment, they seemed to crystallize the paths of all life's searching.

I respected my mind. I wanted to clearly, logically, truly think through every line of my philosophy. I was studying intently toward that goal. But, as I curled up on the bed with my diary, I perceived that although all of that mental activity was worthy, valuable, important . . . it was not *the* essential. If all the excellent arguments remained clothed in black and white in philosophy books, I still would remain personally *alone.*

It was only as the arguments stepped into the Personality who would constantly companion me in the flux of life's changing seasons that I would find the courage to stand.

I determined that I would ever strive to walk in widening dimension through the door of intellectual knowledge . . . but more . . . I would ever strive to, moment-by-moment, expand my repertoire of experiential knowledge by "practicing His presence" . . . on mountaintops . . . in valleys . . . on awakening . . . in sleeping . . . and in all the occasions in-between.

I kept that resolve.

Today there are many facets of knowledge about God that I *intellectually know* . . .

There are many facets of knowledge about God that I *intellectually do not know* . . . because the mystery of the Almighty is ever-present.

Today there are many facets of knowledge about God that I *experientially know* . . . gained in living every moment of every day of every year with Him . . . practicing His presence . . . proving His reality.

These two doors stand ajar for your entrance. Enter each with full-hearted endeavor.

One is important;
    the other vital.
Explore in the one;
    daily *live* in the other.

In the knowledge you gain through these two doors you will find guidance for all of the future.

That is your security as you poise in the Beginning of Becoming . . . with God!

That He Will Never Let Me Go

It is life.
Constantly-changing . . .
       ever-orbiting . . .
              ceaselessly transforming . . .
I have experiential knowledge that, in each season, in each time under the heavens, God will be near me always and He will never let me go.

When springtime tripped about the earth, the woods sprouted feathers of green and the ground came alive with the joy of growing things. My heart drank in the sweetness of honeysuckle blooms. Standing in the midst of so much splendor, it was easy to see God's hand.

I could see purpose in life when my boughs held dancing leaves. I could see destiny when my bright green hedge made a border of beauty to hold those I loved. I could see design when billowy summer clouds skipped joyously across an azure sky. It was easy to give thanks then.

Even in autumn, when summer was dying and the maples burned with brilliant color, I savored the fleeting beauty and gave thanks. Each season had held its own peculiar charm and each had seemed to give thanks to the Creator in its own way.

But now it is winter. Standing beneath the tall trees in

my yard, I see they have shed the last gold leaf, yet their barren arms stretch toward leaden skies in thanksgiving. The hedge about my yard has caught the drifts of dry leaves in its warm embrace, and seems to whisper, "Let us give thanks."

Here in the wintry bleakness, sensing nature's song of gratitude, I smile and whisper, "I, too, give thanks in winter."

I have known springtime and beauty and laughter and have felt keenly the presence of God. But I have seen the springtime of life give way to the heat of summer and the beauty of autumn. I have shivered in the howling winds of winter. Then were my eyes blinded by the hard glitter oi icy fields scoured bright as armor and steely hard as hate. My heart was chilled.

But even then, when there seemed nothing left to hope for, I knew that the hand of my heavenly Father was lovingly at work in my behalf. I saw that He had a purpose when my mind could find no reason for the emptiness of my boughs. I trusted His wisdom when I could not hedge out the darkness from those I loved. I saw God at work when every cloud in my darkened sky was torn and broken. Lifting my soul above the cold, dead winter of life, I worshiped.

When it is wintertime in the symphony of the seasons, nature still sings, even though her music is slower and more subdued than in the joyful spring. I, who have learned her lesson, pause in the gathering darkness and join her prayer.

Oh God, Your love is beautiful in spring when the orchards give their fragrant promise of fruit in summer. I gather Your love to my heart and cry out with rapture for all the joys with which my life is filled. I thank You for Your love in springtime . . . and summer . . . and autumn. . . .

But now winter is here.

The orchards are bare, and all is cold and dark and dead; yet I find Your love equally magnificent. In the drab wintertime of life, I have found Your love full of comfort and warmth like a glowing fireside. It brings new challenge, new hope into the darkened chambers of my heart. It makes my heart a sanctuary wherein dwells the quiet strength of the holy place. It promises another spring, and with the promise come direction and courage to begin again . . . for I am never alone!

There are always two of us involved: God, the Creator
I, the created . . .

You are my Constant Companion.
There is no need that You cannot fulfill.
Whether your course for me points
   to the mountaintops of glorious ecstasy
   or to the valleys of human suffering,
You are by my side.
You are ever-present with me.
You are close beside me
   when I tread the dark streets of danger,
   and even when I flirt with death itself,
You will not leave me.
When the pain is severe,
   You are near to comfort.
When the burden is heavy,
   You are there to lean upon.
When depression darkens my soul,
   You touch me with eternal joy.
When I feel empty and alone,

94

You fill the aching vacuum with Your power.
My security is in Your promise
to be near me always . . .
and in the knowledge
That You will never let me go.*

Ah, Father God . . . through all life's changing seasons, I have seen Your hand at work, Your love revealed, Your redemption in operation . . .

I have known Your constant presence fulfilling every need . . .

For this I thank You . . . and pray that it may ever be thus . . .
Until earth's seasons cease
for me and I awake

in Your likeness
in another world.
For I have the knowledge
that in this world or the next
I shall never be alone.
You will never let me go.

This is the essence of security for all God's beloved children . . . and, perhaps, in a divinely-special way for *you* as you poise at the Beginning of Becoming . . . with God!

*Adapted from PSALSM/NOW, Leslie F. Brandt.